KANSAS CITY GOTHIC

Alex Tretbar is a Midwestern writer and abolitionist. He is also the author of the chapbook *According to the Plat Thereof* (Ethel, 2025), and works in the Center for Digital and Public Humanities at the University of Missouri-Kansas City, where he is currently studying the archive of early issues of *New Letters* (1934-1951) and assisting with the Kansas City Monuments Coalition.

ISBN: 978-1-917617-38-3

Cover designed by Aaron Kent

Edited and Typeset by Aaron Kent

Broken Sleep Books Ltd
PO BOX 102
Llandysul
SA44 9BG

PRAISE for *Kansas City Gothic*

Alex Tretbar's *Kansas City Gothic* simultaneously maps bodies full of hunger, full of longing, while engaging slyly and philosophically with enclosures and landscapes. Where at first the bodies feel either trapped in the carceral establishment or within their own addictive impulses, soon—through language—they give way to varied sites of being and creation. This preternatural legerdemain is accomplished through deft verbal dexterity that lives in form and breaks form. Outward hunger manifests and—ouroboros-like—turns back: "I saw in the concave calcium mirror / that I had become my own food / supply, self-cannibal: / a lidless eye of only pupil." The magic of this poetry reaches beyond the speaker's dense meditations on self to include engagements with others on the fringes, where the "you" proliferates to "represent three / or more discrete dead friends" as another speaker asks "*what physical changes can I expect / to see when nearing death* in the shadow / of dwarf's owl clover and spruce"; here is a fierce ideological critique of America that is both fugue and toccata, where the poet holds up fractured mirrors to the self and the world. I have read nothing like Tretbar, nothing that combines the body politic with the body aesthetic. *Kansas City Gothic* is the beginning of a singular new voice in contemporary poetry.
— Charles Kell

In musical notation, a coda designates the final part of a piece. "But there is no finality here," I thought as Alex Tretbar's *Kansas City Gothic* devoured me. Music came to mind repeatedly: music and memory fashioned with an unrelenting, brilliant intensity. From the dialectic energy of the titling to his conceptual engagement of the Great American Songbook, Tretbar startles and stuns. He lyricizes the line break's relation to time. He calls us into the aural texture of the carceral phone call—"the silence would just elongate, distend"—and blazes the contrast between "fast-food" and waiting for drugs or deliverance. Images strike the eye and ear simultaneously, as with the "cornflower blue I remember" and the use of reverse anaphora. The book you are holding contains one of the best sonnet coronas I've ever read; its flowers still shimmer and take up space in the crannies of my head. I can *hear* them, just as I hear Kansas City, the plains narrowing the horizon and marking the spaces where "every *hello*" is "preauthorized," packaged by U.S. socialization, for the given material world includes the commodified emptiness that shines at its center. Tretbar's critique of carceral systems feels almost Proustian: it is built into the alternating structure between "Movement" and "Coda," redbricked into the longing for home, justice, and hope. There are so many ways to be destroyed by late capitalism. Tretbar's poems admit this. Yet they resist all foregone conclusiveness in their insistent use of the lyric to reimagine hope and possibility. The stories we tell, the music (and muses) of self-narration, the treasured spaces kept secret in the landscapes which shaped us: all meet in these extraordinary pieces and poems. Truly astonished by the skill of these poems, and how intimately Tretbar's hand knows the lyre it holds.
— Alina Stefanescu

Contents

Kansas City Gothic

Alex Tretbar

Broken Sleep Books

MOVEMENT

i.

The dead sun's necklace is what I remember

most, the conspiracy of hawthorn converging on Troost Avenue, the redbrick

songbook of a spiral mirror. Have you been caressed by your own food supply?

Have you descended the cane of the rose down into your navel? Did you bleed

enough? The wrecking ball slick with albumen destroys no matter

which way it turns for help, and the addicted father in the park screams

Swing batter, swing. It's hard to ignore crabapples when they have your name

written on them, when they have been airborne since 1897. I used to be home

-less, too. Every *hello* I entertained was preauthorized, and I would pitch

my hammock between two yews above the sidewalk. Hell turned out to be a breeze

-way between two heavens, but I settled for a crumb of angel food.

CODA

This is the silver

cornflower blue I remember, the dog-day

cicadas hypnotized by their own plainsong

and the puppy star barking

from behind my uvula, mouth

filling with the black gold

Achilles' mother dipped him in

each morning, my own mother's white noise

machine protecting her sleep

from me, and how I woke at the southern

terminus of Rainbow Boulevard

ii.

the terminus of Rainbow Boulevard

gets lost in throats of country

clubs and the shallow, broken neck

of Brush Creek, traditional Latin

Mass harmonizing with the photon

beams of Westwood Radiology

at this nexus of wealth and malaise

crowned by tasteless stonecrop

older now and place-weary I realize

our sickness is a standard

in the Great American Songbook

iii.

in the Great American Songbook

I hail Cole Porter

trickster in pain perpetual

upon whom Plymouth Rock landed

like a ton of bricks on sick leave

and as for him so for me: *anything goes*

in the Great American Songbook

where 57 songs begin with "I":

"I Fall in Love Too Easily"

"I Want to Be Happy"

"I Could Write a Book"

iv.

I could write a book

about Kansas City as the egg

I woke up as a quiche within

after the steppe of a juniper spiral

staircase under Oregon

and found I was no longer bathed

and caressed by the nutrient

I saw in the concave calcium mirror

that I had become my own food

supply, self-cannibal:

a lidless eye of only pupil

v.

a lidless eye of only pupil

composite shoe and star and navel

gazer, I blur my self as I approach

the rose that climbed my Skid Row

window in search of succor

from the street, I add a supermodel

polish to the demolished building

I used to buy dope in front of, I bought it

from Wheelchair Tony, his rope of gin-spittle

swinging like the grandfather pendulum

of a handless water clock

vi.

like a handless water clock

I carom coinlike between 200 fountains

wetting the tongues of thirsty dogs and birds

and horses whinnying at my barred window

in the Vine Street workhouse castle

1897, a politics of Ben Day dots

gathering where I sprawl out on a hay

mattress, behouseflied beneath the comic strip

caption: *A grand cleaning up of hoboes*

and hoboesses, the castellated towers

in vogue in this part of my mind

vii.

in vogue in this part of my mind

is the way the free answer the phone

because when the imprisoned calls from prison

the burden of the first hello for some reason

rests on the caller's tongue, my thesis for the phenomenon being

the called party is never really sure it's you, is always hesitant

to begin a conversation with the potentially dead or suddenly

changed, and so the called party waits, and I found that if I didn't break
the silence

the silence would just elongate, distend, the called party unwilling to disturb

their own disturbance, so that even now when I call a dentist or a doctor

it takes everything in me not to say *hello*

viii.

it takes everything in me not to say *hello*

to the man in the park devouring a northern wind

through a test tube from which the blue silk rose

was removed upon purchase to make room

for the moth-gray pebble, above him the yew

needles hiding the arils hiding the poison

of the seed, and wordless I sit down

without guile or weapon

and recalibrate the rabbit ears of his cardboard TV

to October 3rd, 1960—the yews watching us

watching the Andy Griffith Show premiere

ix.

watching the Andy Griffith Show premiere

I can almost hear

the five-year-empty hole in my arm

sighing in time with the laugh track

and the piano-key blinds the wind plays

when mother leaves a crack in the sliding

glass door open, I can't decide which year

I want to live in, maybe none, maybe years

are for the birds, and in the end I am just my father

again, drinking milk with a medium-rare steak

patiently waiting for the angel food

x.

patiently waiting for the angel food

to alight in the smoky den

on a plate the same color

as a Wichita dawn: silver

cornflower blue, gold-inlaid

halo round the food

stabilized by cream

of tartar, is there

a powder

side-effectless

to stabilize me, too

xi.

to stabilize me, too—

that's all I was trying to do

I pulled into the fast-food lot

and waited for 6 hours

at one point spending 1 of my 21

dollars on a soda, leaving intact the price

of admission to heavenhell, the demarcation

dreamed up by those who've never been there:

where the protein is fried in Lethe

and the newest moons of tar

comprise the Kids Meals

MOVEMENT

ii.

White cake morsel in the halo's bullseye: Kids Meal for cherubim.

Let's hum a hymn: for the punk lofts extant only in fisheye photos,

the hothouse sunflowers on the moon's to-do list, and the plexiglass raincoat

my personality's kernel wore to the wake. I've pitched a tarp to stave

off multiplicity, but ponderosas fracture their collarbones toasting the sky.

What if the reason Narcissus couldn't look away was that his hideousness

mesmerized him? Ill aesthetes, we load up beheading videos midwinter

when blood and sand play perfect foil to the permafrost of Arrowhead

Stadium. We slow down the car crash and look for ourselves

among the survivors: an errant bluish constellation begging for medicine.

Yes, I am always on time. I'm saving all of my sick days for the catastrophe.

CODA

an adult buys a Kids Meal

and promptly throws away

everything but the Pikachu

who is happy to see me (and I

am, too!) the red suns of its cheeks

rising, now setting, ears at 12 and 2

p.m. on the clocktower of my youth

presiding over the heart's red plaza

where I beg the passing blood cells

for spare change to buy a pack of

the cigarettes that will kill them

xiii.

the cigarettes that will kill them

burn in constellative devotion

along the sidewalk in front of the Studded

Bird, punk space now buried by the tent

and awning company, the brassworks wall

of the power plant across the street, no tree

in sight, the dead lens of sky engraving

our image in fisheye starlight: this

is two thousand eleven, and I am holed

up in a Xanax pillbox

tuning my bass to a sharp heaven

xiv.

tuning my bass to a sharp heaven

somewhere east of middle C

261.625565 hertz

where nothing hurts

not even the red-hot needle

stitching a seam of black

sunflowers along the equator

of my whitening pupil

in the sun's darkroom / cloakroom

and I can no longer remember

who I gave my coat to

xv.

I give my coat to

the officer who escorts me

to a plexiglass wall on the other side

of which a different officer tells me

my charges are mandatory

minimum sentence charges

adding up to 160 months

and 13 months later I'm offered

the coat which no longer fits

because I gained 30 pounds

waiting to go to prison

xvi.

waiting to go to prison

is pitching a tent

beyond metonymy

where all I mean by cage

is cage and its only perfect rhyme

is age: how can a memory

embody a multiplicity

of event, a raindrop

remember the sea

and its own extinction

its drought

xvii.

its drought

this red equinox

this "artist's bracket and allies"

Ganoderma sessile

inventing civilization

in the ponderosa clavicle, this pine

I pause before at dawn

and lose myself in the colony

of hyphae dying for lack of water

this lack of water

I feel but cannot prove

xviii.

I feel but cannot prove

that all of my songs are about you

and the unlocked cells of your body

warmed by Indian blanket

and cardinal flowers on the threshold

of your speechless winter

how I tracked the pinemoths

migrating from your stomach

through nasogastric tubes

in a light-winged hush

to silence the world

xix.

to silence the world

I stopper the aperture of Arrowhead Stadium

I stopper the sky with my own closed eyes

I stopper the cup of coffee with my hand

I stopper the sound hole of the guitar choked with catgut

I stopper the boredom with abject stimuli

I stopper at the stop sign in time to not get stoppered myself

I stopper the thoughts I drink about you every day

I stopper the amber vial of amyl nitrite

that allowed me to speak to you

in tongues, after your death

xx.

in tongues, after your death

in the face of oncoming

traffic, I braid a rope

of the tongues of all friends

I've lost, and when plaited

they don't sound all that different

from the million flatted thirds

harmonizing in a slowed-down car

crash, its metallurgic deconstruction

over which presides the tastefully lit

accursed four-blade star

xxi.

the accursed four-blade star

under which presides the tastefully lit

Accurso Law Firm, I was encouraged

to walk here hours before dawn, to the Cancer

Survivors Park, to sit on a curved plank bench among greenery

only to find that a couple with a bottle have beaten me here

to toast their immortality before a monument to mortality

so I walk through the groves of statuary in search of another

place to exist, another alcove, but a pillow comes into view

and a sound comes into hearing: flick of a dead lighter

and by the spark of the flint I can see he is blind

xxii.

by the spark of the flint I can see he is blind

but doesn't need my help to stir the cold heroin

so I move on to the undesirable quarter

of the monument, its streetward openness

and voyeurism, its throning of you

as a bullseye in the headlights

of every passing car, and have you ever

done as I have done, looked up half-lidded

and mistaken a spray of spruce

for an errant bluish constellation

they didn't teach us about in school

MOVEMENT

iii.

I called in sick at the first sign of unintelligible bellowing. Cashed out

my 401(k) in non-psychoactive candy. Now, in a sandbox at the end

of all starlight, I trace concentric circles with a rod of iron. Earth its own

hospice, gathered around its bedside with offerings of spruce and clover. Even
>   when

the city's population dwindled to one, I didn't stop barking. A mayfly barreled
>   through

May, leaving an exit wound. The Missouri is the Willamette is the Los Angeles.

I dodo the mass grave named after an insurance company, but place seems
>   unimportant

all of a sudden, despite my present devotion to it. What if the prodigal son had
>   returned

to a scorched farm? Would the fattened calf have cut its own throat? The key
>   to the cell

reads *do not duplicate*, but it has been duplicated. The morning sky is a fist of
>   lapis lazuli

mounted in a sterling bezel. It both is and absorbs light. The dead sun wears it.

CODA

xxiii.

they didn't teach me in school

about how "you" can represent three

or more discrete dead friends

one of whom was almost me

on a paid-leave workday downtown

at the infamous wall with fist-sized holes

I passed my hundred dollars through

oh ramparts between health and sickness

I took a knee in your dust and blessed

the star winking out in your medicine

I sipped from the dipper of fentanyl

xxiv.

I sipped from the dipper of fentanyl

like the guy I knew who sucked a lollipop

a hundred times stronger than morphine

lying with his daughter on the living room floor

and in the blue aftermath we thanked Dora

the Explorer for discovering the body

before it could remake itself into a white dwarf

and I want to tell you that his daughter was sad

when we pulled her from the circle

of her father's arms, but she was laughing

as she reached for the bright and hidden candy

xxv.

she reached for the bright and hidden candy

on the top shelf between God's eyeteeth

and the ladder fell away

and she, not falling, rose

into the understanding

that place is far

less important

than books

would have you believe

and twelve years later she is still

drawing circles in the sand

xxvi.

drawing circles in the sand

still others leave amid a circle

of loving faces around their bedsides

at Kansas City Hospice where I ask

what physical changes can I expect

to see when nearing death in the shadow

of dwarf owl's clover and spruce

across the street is Kansas

but I'm standing in Missouri

watching a man on the telephone pole

avoid electrocution

xxvii.

avoid electrocution

I overhear the spray paint say

to the abutment of the bridge as I approach

Brush Creek, cool brown tributary

of the Blue beside whose mayfly / stonefly /

caddisfly-woven surface a youth sleeps with *The Broom*

of the System as their pillow on the metal

bench, and I pause pause pause

I almost pause to take a picture

of their sleep, their hot oblivion

in the dead dog days of summer

xxviii.

in the dead dog days of summer

I cross the little bridges with my eyes

buried in my sunburned hands, remembering

PDX crypted by snow December '16

the complicit Hawthorne Bridge

the addict leaping to her life

rewriting history in the river

and I'm shaken awake by freshwater sweat

I wring my sunbaked cerements

in the locked taupe closets

these backrooms of the watershed

xxix.

these backrooms of the watershed

this coffee-web of the Mississippi watershed:

in one of these backrooms all of my selves convene

to weave a hushed conspiracy of place

and we find we cannot turn

our backs to the gadwalls on the stream

and I find I have to turn

away from the Boston ivy of the retaining wall

my back up against it I fall into disrepair

oh body I've tried to keep you satisfied I've tried

to limit your multiplication

xxx.

to limit your multiplication

quell the impulse to echo

Sevillian architecture

do not overplan the erection

of one of the world's sixty

great places, ignore the destinied

manifest trailing its erection afield

and when shoppers arrive by car

give them instead of tradable wares

a vantage, a black inverted flower

itching for the head's twin exit wounds

xxxi.

itching for the head's twin exit wounds

and what their entered eyes are not unable to not unsee

I suggest you *contact the administration directly*

to find out if an inmate you know

is in the facility by phone 816-881-4200

and I recommend coming to early terms

with the maze's outward order

its red and vertiginous panoptical beauty

distilled imperfectly in the logo of its app

an ice-blue aegis *which is found*

a traffic light away from the prison

xxxii.

a traffic light away from the prison

I step from the nave of St. Mary's

out onto 13th and to the east

is George Brett Super Highway, aorta

of the 192-atom loop where 70

and 670 and 71 and 40

get lost in each other's throats

and end up found in mine:

singer astonished by coda

this is the silver

cornflower blue I remember

xxxiii.

the silver cornflower blue I remember

the dead sun's necklace I remember

the nothingness of all rivers I remember

the unabridged beheadings I remember

I thread my head through the bezel I remember

the Missouri is the Willamette I remember

the million keys to the million cells I remember

the juniper spiral staircase I remember

is there a room beyond medicine I remember

rounding the bend, the scorched farm I remember

I am, and absorb, light I remember

NOTES

Page 7: Troost Avenue is named after Dr. Benoist Troost (1786-1859), "Kansas City's first physician" and a known enslaver. Community efforts to rename the street have repeatedly been met with inaction by the city (https://www.startlandnews.com/2025/05/troost-truth/).

Page 13: "…a grand cleaning up of hoboes and hoboesses" is taken from "Ready for Its Hobo Guests," published in *The Kansas City Star* on December 20, 1897.

Page 35: "…still others leave amid a circle of loving faces around their bedsides" and "what physical changes can I expect to see when nearing death" are both taken from the website of Kansas City Hospice and Palliative Care (https://www.kchospice.org/family/caregiver-tips/when-death-nears/).

Page 39: Project for Public Spaces lists the Country Club Plaza as one of "60 of the World's Great Places," and describes it as "[t]he world's first (1922) and probably best shopping center built to accommodate the auto" (https://www.pps.org/article/60places). The Country Club Plaza is essentially an outdoor mall, from which small and local businesses have largely been banished. Planned and developed by J.C. Nichols, it is "inspired by the grand plazas of Spain and features distinctive Spanish Revival architecture with terracotta roofs, intricate tilework, and lush courtyards" (https://countryclubplaza.com/about/). Nichols (1880-1950) was an urban planner who sought to enforce racial segregation and redlining in Kansas City. Nichols' "Country Club District," as it was initially called, came with a detailed list of requirements for home builders and buyers, among which was included the provision "OWNERSHIP BY NEGROES PROHIBITED" (https://www.kansascity.com/news/local/article247787885.html). The Dallas retail company HP Village Management purchased the Plaza in 2024; one of the company's leaders, Heather Hill Washburne, "is a prominent fundraiser for the Republican Party and was a member of former President Donald Trump's intelligence advisory board" (KCUR). In May 2025, HP Village Management announced that it would be stepping up security and surveillance in the Plaza: armed Class A security guards capable of detaining civilians; increased presence of Kansas City Police Department patrol officers and patrol cars; new cameras and "enhanced technology" upgrades to existing cameras (https://fox4kc.com/news/armed-security-guards-heading-to-kcs-country-club-plaza-via-new-owners/).

Page 40: "…contact the administration directly to find out if an inmate you know is in the facility by phone 816-881-4200" and "which is found a traffic light away from the prison" are both taken from online information regarding the Jackson County Regional Detention Center.

ACKNOWLEDGMENTS

"Coda" i., ii., xxix., and xxx. first appeared in *New Critique*.

"Coda" xviii., xix., xxiv., and xxv. first appeared in *Ocean State Review*.

Thank you first and foremost to my mother, without whose living room and air mattress I would not have been able to write this book in the initial months after my release from prison in July 2022. **Thank you, too, to the rest of my family.**

I am grateful for everyone whose support in various ways made this book possible, including but not limited to: Irene Cooper, Mike Cooper, Laura Winberry, Carrie Walker, Angela Madden, Anita Goodwin, Janet Narum, Johnny Stallings, Joseph Byrd, Steve Maack, Brian Daldorph, Charles Kell, Matthew Denis, Austin Holland, Eric Martinez, Sam Sarsten, Randy Ewing, Jeff Kuehner, Alexander Maycher, Crystal Rhoades, Benjamin Onkka, Pam Wingo, John Wingo, Shannon Grindinger, Thom Eichelberger-Young, and Elise Tran, my partner in time and space.

Thank you, too, to Aaron Kent and the entire Broken Sleep team.

This book is dedicated to the addicted, and to everyone living in prison or on the streets.

LAY OUT YOUR UNREST

www.ingramcontent.com/pod-product-compliance
Lightning Source LLC
La Vergne TN
LVHW041310080426
835510LV00009B/943

9 7 8 1 9 1 7 6 1 7 3 8 3